Moon Landings

By Shoshana Z. Weider

Editors Kathleen Teece, Kritika Gupta
Senior Art Editor Jim Green
Project Art Editor Lucy Sims
Art Editor Kanika Kalra
Jacket Coordinator Francesca Young
Jacket Designer Suzena Sengupta
DTP Designers Ashok Kumar, Dheeraj Singh
Picture Researcher Sakshi Saluja
Producer, Pre-Production Rob Dunn
Senior Producer Isabell Schart
Managing Editors Laura Gilbert, Monica Saigal
Managing Art Editor Diane Peyton Jones
Deputy Managing Art Editor Ivy Sengupta
Delhi Team Head Malavika Talukder
Creative Director Helen Senior
Publishing Director Sarah Larter

Reading Consultant Linda Gambrell
Educational Consultant Jacqueline Harris

First published in Great Britain in 2019
by Dorling Kindersley Limited
80 Strand, London, WC2R 0RL

A CIP catalogue record for this book
is available from the British Library.
ISBN: 978-0-2413-5853-5

Printed and bound in China

The publisher would like to thank the following for their kind permission to reproduce their photographs:
(Key: a-above; b-below/bottom; c-centre; f-far; l-left; r-right; t-top)

1 NASA. 3 Dreamstime.com: Scol22 (br/Moon). **NASA:** (br). **5 123RF.com:** pockygallery. **6–7 NASA. 9 NASA. 10–11 NASA:** Reid Wiseman (@astro_reid). **11 Getty Images:** Detlef van Ravenswaay (b). **12 Alamy Stock Photo:** ITAR-TASS News Agency (cr, bl). **12–13 Depositphotos Inc:** Helen_F (Border). **Dreamstime.com:** Andreykuzmin. **13 Getty Images:** Bettmann (bl). **NASA:** (tl, cr). **14 Getty Images:** Ralph Morse / The LIFE Picture Collection. **15 NASA. 16 Alamy Stock Photo:** NASA Image Collection. **19 NASA. 20 NASA. 22–23 Getty Images:** SSPL. **24–25 Depositphotos Inc:** Helen_F (Border). **27 Alamy Stock Photo:** Science History Images (b). **NASA:** (tr). **28–29 Dreamstime.com:** Scol22. **NASA:** (Crew members). **30–31 Dreamstime.com:** Lavendertime (t/Sky). **NASA:** (t). **32 NASA. 33 Getty Images:** Otis Imboden / National Geographic. **35 NASA. 36–37 NASA. 39 NASA:** Johnson Space Center. **40 NASA:** Moss (b). **Dee O'Hara:** NASA (cl). **41 Alamy Stock Photo:** Archive PL (cl); ZUMA Press, Inc. (t). **NASA:** Langley Research Center (br). **43 NASA. 44–45 NASA:** (t). **45 NASA:** (br). **46 NASA. 48–49 NASA. 50 Science Photo Library:** NASA. **51 NASA:** Johnson Space Center Gateway to Astronaut Photography of Earth. **52–53 NASA. 54 NASA. 54–55 Depositphotos Inc:** Helen_F (Border). **55 Science Photo Library:** Mark Williamson (br). **56–57 Depositphotos Inc:** Helen_F (Border). **56 ESA:** (br). **Rex by Shutterstock:** Sipa Press (cl). **57 Getty Images:** Pallava Bagla / Corbis (clb). **Japan Aerospace Exploration Agency (JAXA):** (t). **58–59 Depositphotos Inc:** Helen_F (Border). **60–61 Depositphotos Inc:** Helen_F (Border). **62–63 Depositphotos Inc:** Helen_F (Border)

Endpaper images: Front: **NASA**; Back: **NASA**

Cover images: Front: **123RF.com:** Peter Jurik c; **Dreamstime.com:** Forplayday t; **NASA**; Back: **Dreamstime.com:** Forplayday tl

All other images © Dorling Kindersley
For further information see: www.dkimages.com

A WORLD OF IDEAS:
SEE ALL THERE IS TO KNOW

www.dk.com

Contents

4   Chapter 1: The Moon and space travel

12   *Important figures*

14   Chapter 2: Going to the Moon

24   *Apollo spacecraft*

26   Chapter 3: Apollo 11

40   *Women of Apollo*

42   Chapter 4: After the first landing

54   *Lunar rovers*

56   *Recent international Moon explorations*

58   Quiz

60   Glossary

62   Index

Chapter 1
The Moon and space travel

The Moon has fascinated people for thousands of years. It is the Earth's satellite, which means it constantly orbits (circles) our planet.

The Moon was important in many ancient religions. People would hold festivals when the full Moon shone at certain times during the year. The ancient Greeks believed that a Moon goddess called Phoebe dragged it into the sky each night with her chariot.

We know that the Moon is extremely ancient – about 4.5 billion years old.

This is almost as old as the Earth. Scientists believe the Moon formed when the Earth and another body crashed into each other. The debris from the collision formed the Moon.

The Earth and its Moon.

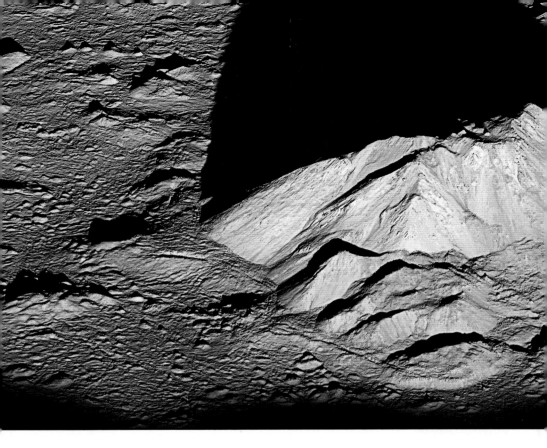

The Moon is the brightest object we see in the night sky. Sometimes it is even visible during the day. We only ever see one side of the Moon as it travels around the Earth.

The Moon is a rocky body covered in craters and mountains. From the Earth, we see darker and lighter spots.

The central peak of the
Moon's Tycho crater.

The dark areas are craters filled with
a type of rock called basalt. The lighter
areas are the mountains, made from
a paler rock, known as anorthosite.

There is no atmosphere or liquid
water on the Moon's surface. This
means that no animals or plants
can live there.

Our journey to the Moon began when humans sent an object into space for the first time. This was a German V-2 rocket, launched on 20 June, 1944. The rocket reached a height of 176 kilometres (109 miles) above the Earth. Yet, this was still a huge distance from the Moon.

After World War II, many of the engineers who built the V-2 rockets moved to the USA. The rockets were soon made to be better and more powerful. Many exciting V-2 missions were carried out. In 1947, living creatures were sent into space for the first time inside a V-2. These were tiny fruit flies!

A US rocket that used parts of the V-2, Bumper 2, was launched from Cape Canaveral, Florida, USA, in July 1950.

After 1945 there was a tense period between the USA and the Soviet Union (now Russia). The two nations began competing to be first to send people into space. This was the start of the "Space Race".

In 1957, the Soviets were the first to put an object into orbit around the Earth.

The world's first artificial satellite, Sputnik 1, was the size of a beachball. It orbited the Earth for three months.

This small metal satellite was called Sputnik 1. In 1959, the Soviets also landed the first robotic probe on the Moon's surface.

The Russians' next achievement was even more daring. On 12 April, 1961, cosmonaut Yuri Gagarin became the first person in space. He made one orbit of the Earth in the Vostok 1 spacecraft.

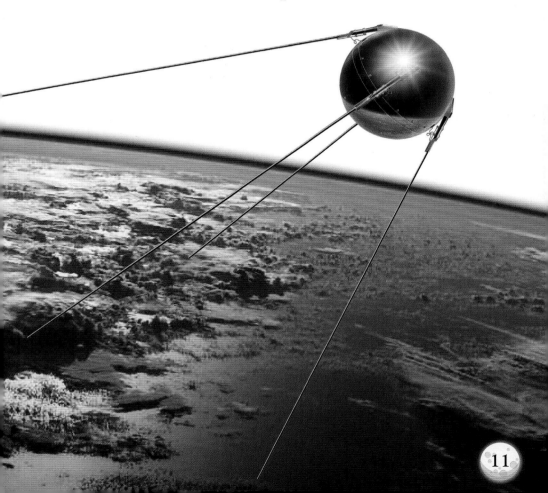

Important figures

These are some of the many scientists and engineers whose work helped us to develop successful missions to the Moon.

Konstantin Tsiolkovsky

Born: 1857
Died: 1935
Nationality: Russian

Tsiolkovsky wrote one of the first books that used science and maths to explain how rockets could travel to space.

Valentina Tereshkova

Born: 1937
Nationality: Russian

Originally an engineer, cosmonaut Tereshkova was the first woman to fly in space. She orbited the Earth in Vostok 6, in 1963.

Wernher von Braun

Born: 1912
Died: 1977
Nationality: German

Von Braun played an important role in the design of rockets for NASA, including the Saturn V vehicle for the Apollo missions.

John C. Houbolt

Born: 1919
Died: 2014
Nationality: American

Houbolt helped to plan the "lunar-orbit-rendezvous" method for landing humans on the Moon. This was used in the Apollo missions.

Robert Goddard

Born: 1882
Died: 1945
Nationality: American

Goddard created and launched the world's first liquid-fuelled rocket. His ideas and inventions helped develop modern rockets for long-distance spaceflights.

Chapter 2
Going to the Moon

The US president John F. Kennedy made a bold move in May 1961. This was shortly after Alan Shepard had become the first American to go to space. Kennedy promised to land a man on the Moon and return him safely to the Earth before 1970. Americans started to make new programmes that would send more missions to space. These were controlled by NASA, which is the American space agency.

Alan Shepard

NASA was soon sending astronauts into orbit around the Earth and robotic probes to the Moon.

To land humans on the Moon, NASA created the Apollo programme. However, in January 1967 there was a tragic fire during training for the first Apollo mission. It killed all three of the crew.

President Kennedy giving his "We choose to go to the Moon" speech at the Rice Stadium, Texas, in September 1962.

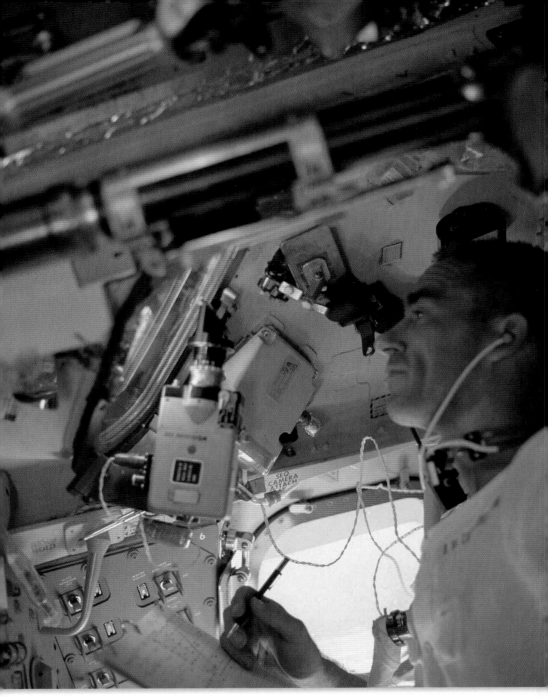

Lunar Module Pilot Walt Cunningham inside
the Apollo 7 Command and Service Module.

Apollo 7 was the first successful crewed Apollo mission. It was launched in October 1968. Wally Schirra, Donn Eisele and Walt Cunningham were the astronauts. They spent 11 days orbiting the Earth. Life inside the spacecraft was very cramped. Because there was no gravity, the astronauts could float around. However, there was little room to move or exercise.

The astronauts slept in a section of Apollo 7 called the Command and Service Module, strapped onto their couches. They also ate three freeze-dried meals there each day.

All three astronauts came down with a flu-like illness. This could have been a cold that spread between them in the tiny space!

Apollo 8 was the next mission. It took place during December 1968. Launched on a hugely powerful Saturn V rocket, it was the first Apollo mission to travel all the way to the Moon.

The Apollo 8 astronauts, Frank Borman, Jim Lovell and Bill Anders, were the first humans to get far enough from the Earth to see the whole sphere of our planet. They also witnessed a beautiful "earthrise" from lunar orbit.

The astronauts made an emotional television broadcast on Christmas Eve. Viewers on the Earth watched in awe as the astronauts flew their spacecraft over the Moon's barren surface.

A photograph of the "earthrise" taken by Bill Anders, from Apollo 8.

A photograph of Dave Scott taken by astronaut Rusty Schweickart during the spacewalk.

Apollo 9 took place in March 1969. It was the first time that the Lunar Module was tested in space. This was the part of the Apollo spacecraft that would eventually take astronauts all the way to the Moon's surface.

The Apollo 9 astronauts spent 10 days orbiting the Earth. They practised separating the Command and Service Module and the Lunar Module. The two sections of the spacecraft were flown more than 175 kilometres (110 miles) apart and brought back together again.

During the mission, Rusty Schweickart performed a "spacewalk". He spent 37 minutes outside the spacecraft. Imagine floating in space and looking down on the Earth!

Apollo 10 was the final rehearsal for landing people on the Moon. Astronauts Tom Stafford, John Young and Gene Cernan lifted off on their Saturn V rocket on 18 May, 1969.

Four days later, Stafford and Cernan flew the Lunar Module to within 16 kilometres (10 miles) of the lunar surface. Young stayed in the Command and Service Module orbiting the Moon.

The Lunar Module was tiny. It had extremely thin walls and three small windows. To make it as light as possible, there were no seats. The astronauts used aircraft-like hand controllers to pilot the Lunar Module.

It looked like the USA would win the Space Race, but the Soviets were also still hard at work. They continued to send probes into orbit around the Moon.

Apollo spacecraft

The spacecraft that sent astronauts to the Moon, and brought them back to the Earth, were made up of several different parts. The rocket that carried them to space was called Saturn V.

Lunar Module descent stage: Contained the engine for landing, and carried the ascent stage away from the Moon.

Apollo spacecraft

Lunar Module ascent stage: The crew's cabin and control room. Upon leaving the Moon, it separated from the descent stage.

Landing pad

Command Module:
Housed the astronauts for most of their journey. It was the only section to splashdown in the ocean.

Parachute

Fuel tank

The Apollo spacecraft mounted on the Saturn V rocket.

Service Module: Included engines and fuel tanks needed to power the rocket, plus room to store equipment.

Massive and extremely powerful Saturn V rockets were used to launch all Apollo spacecraft. They were more than 100 metres (328 feet) tall.

Chapter 3
Apollo 11

It seemed more and more likely that the US would finally land a man on the Moon. NASA had now shown that they had spacecraft good enough for a mission to the Moon's surface. They were ready to meet the challenge set by President Kennedy back in 1961.

The Apollo 11 mission was scheduled for July 1969. NASA would attempt to land people on the Moon and return them safely to the Earth.

Meanwhile, the Soviets were behind in the Space Race. Their spacecraft and rockets were unreliable. A massive explosion at the Soviet launch facility in July 1969 set them back even further.

The Apollo 11 mission patch was worn by the astronauts on their uniforms.

The Saturn V rocket being assembled.

Apollo 11 was to have a three-person crew. NASA required all early astronauts to be military test pilots. They needed to be comfortable with high-risk flying. Unfortunately, women were disqualified from becoming astronauts because there were no female test pilots at that time.

The astronauts chosen for this mission had performed well on NASA's Gemini spaceflights. Commander Neil Armstrong would be in overall charge of the mission. He and Edwin "Buzz" Aldrin were to land on the lunar surface. Meanwhile, Michael Collins would remain in the Command and Service Module as it orbited the Moon.

Portrait of the Apollo 11 crew –
Neil Armstrong (*left*), Michael
Collins (*centre*) and Edwin
"Buzz" Aldrin (*right*).

All Apollo astronauts completed a tough training programme before their missions. They needed to learn how to control the spacecraft. They practised flying the Lunar Module by piloting the Lunar Landing Research Vehicle.

The Apollo missions would
end when the Command and
Service Module splashed down
in the ocean. The astronauts
were therefore taught to survive
in the water and on desert islands.

The astronauts also studied rock
types. This meant that they could
examine the lunar surface and choose
the best rock samples to bring back
to the Earth for scientific study.

The Saturn V rocket launching with the Apollo 11 crew on 16 July, 1969.

Apollo 11's launch day dawned on 16 July, 1969. More than one million excited people lined the beaches in Florida near the launch site. They were going

Former US President Lyndon B. Johnson and his wife watching the launch of Apollo 11.

to watch the start of a great adventure.

Despite having all the world watching them, the astronauts carefully completed their final tasks. They ate breakfast, put on their spacesuits and made their way to the launchpad at Kennedy Space Center. The countdown had begun.

At nine seconds before launch, Saturn V's five engines ignited. They reached full power at the moment of liftoff – time zero. The huge rocket slowly began to rise, with its roar being heard for hundreds of miles.

Apollo 11 spent two hours orbiting the Earth. It was then sent on its four-day journey to the Moon. It entered lunar orbit at about 100 kilometres (62 miles) above the surface.

The next day, Armstrong and Aldrin entered The Eagle. This was Apollo 11's Lunar Module. They set off on a nerve-racking descent to the lunar surface. Soon, there was only a tiny amount of fuel left! They finally found a safe landing spot and touched down in a huge crater, called the Sea of Tranquillity.

A few hours later, Armstrong stepped onto the Moon. Millions of people watched on television as he famously said, "That's one small step for man, one giant leap for mankind". Buzz Aldrin followed, describing the empty scene as "magnificent desolation".

Buzz Aldrin climbing down the Lunar Module steps to the lunar surface.

Armstrong and Aldrin walked on the Moon for more than two hours. They collected rocks and set up scientific equipment to examine the Moon's surface and interior. They also planted the US flag in the lunar soil. All too soon, it was time to re-enter The Eagle. After resting, the two astronauts flew the craft back to the Command and Service Module.

The historic mission ended on 24 July, 1969 as the spacecraft returned to the Earth. It passed safely through the Earth's atmosphere. Parachutes were then deployed, before the Command and Service Module softly splashed down into the Pacific Ocean.

Astronaut Buzz Aldrin on the Moon with the US flag.

A US Navy ship called the *Hornet* collected the astronauts. They were kept away from other people in case they had brought back diseases from the Moon. US President Richard Nixon welcomed and congratulated them through a glass window. Meanwhile, people around the world joyfully celebrated the successful mission.

The astronauts were in isolation for three weeks. Afterwards, they could finally join the parties being thrown in their honour. They took part in parades around the USA and each astronaut was awarded the Presidential Medal of Freedom. They also received international praise during their 45-day tour of 25 foreign countries.

HORNET + 3

The Apollo 11 astronauts inside the Mobile Quarantine Facility on the *Hornet*, as President Nixon welcomes them back to the Earth on 24 July, 1969.

Women of Apollo

There were no female Apollo astronauts, but women played important roles in getting missions off the ground and to the Moon.

Dee O'Hara
At NASA, O'Hara was the nurse for all the Apollo astronauts.

Billie Robertson
Robertson was a mathematician for NASA. She helped develop computer programs for the Apollo launches.

Poppy Northcutt
Northcutt was the first female engineer to work in NASA's Mission Control.

Katherine Johnson
A brilliant mathematician, Johnson helped figure out the path of Apollo spacecraft. Her work was critical to several NASA missions.

Margaret Hamilton
Hamilton led the team that developed the in-flight software for the Apollo spacecraft.

Chapter 4
After the first landing

Humans had finally landed on the Moon, but there was still a lot more to do up there! More Apollo missions were planned. Apollo 12 flew to the Moon again in November 1969. Pete Conrad and Alan Bean landed their Lunar Module in an area called the Ocean of Storms. They collected part of a probe that had been flown to the Moon in 1967. Scientists wanted to see how it had changed in space.

Some photographs taken by the astronauts on the Moon were lost because Bean accidentally left some of the film there! He later became an artist. He used paint containing Moon dust to draw lunar scenes.

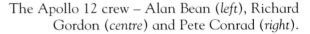

The Apollo 12 crew – Alan Bean (*left*), Richard Gordon (*centre*) and Pete Conrad (*right*).

Apollo 13 lifted off from Florida on 11 April, 1970. It carried astronauts Jim Lovell, Jack Swigert and Fred Haise. Almost 56 hours into their journey to the Moon, however, an explosion happened on board. This caused the spacecraft to quickly lose oxygen and power.

NASA engineers on the Earth had to rapidly plan a rescue mission.

Apollo 13's Jim Lovell, Jack Swigert and Fred Haise on the USS *Iwo Jima* after safely splashing down in the South Pacific Ocean.

They told the astronauts to use the Lunar Module as a lifeboat. The astronauts found their way home by using the position of the stars as a guide. This was a backup method masterminded by mathematician Katherine Johnson. The crew safely splashed down in the South Pacific on 17 April.

Katherine Johnson

NASA did not want another explosion on a spacecraft. They made improvements to the Apollo spacecraft and delayed the launch of Apollo 14 until 31 January, 1971.

The Apollo 14 mission was led by Alan Shepard. He had just recovered from an illness that had almost ended his career. Alan Shepard and Edgar Mitchell stayed on the lunar surface for more than 33 hours. Stuart Roosa remained orbiting the Moon in the Command and Service Module. Shepard and Mitchell explored the Fra Mauro region of the Moon. They collected rock samples and carried out scientific experiments. Shepard even found time to play some golf!

Astronaut Alan Shepard assembling scientific equipment on the Moon.

Apollo 15 was the first in a series of missions designed to stay on the lunar surface for longer. Apollo 15 carried a lunar rover to the Moon for the first time. The astronauts could explore a much larger area with this vehicle.

Astronaut James Irwin saluting the US flag during the moonwalk.

Dave Scott and James Irwin landed near a deep valley, called Hadley Rille, on 30 July, 1971. They collected 77 kilograms (170 pounds) of lunar rocks to bring home. This was much more than from previous missions. The Command and Service Module also carried instruments that studied the lunar surface from orbit.

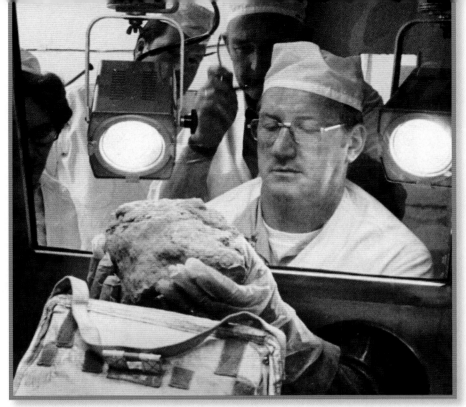

Specialists studying a lunar rock brought back by the Apollo 16 astronauts at the Lunar Receiving Laboratory. This rock is popularly known as "Big Muley".

The last missions to land on the Moon were Apollo 16 and 17 in 1972. Apollo 16's John Young and Charles Duke explored a mountainous area of the Moon. They collected the largest lunar rock sample ever. It weighed almost 12 kilograms (26 pounds).

On the way to the Moon, the Apollo 17 crew snapped a beautiful photograph of the entire Earth. Crew members Gene Cernan and Harrison Schmitt became the last people to walk on the Moon. Before they left, Cernan scratched his daughter's initials, "TDC", into the lunar soil. He wanted it to last for thousands of years.

The "blue marble" photograph of Earth taken by the Apollo 17 crew.

There has been no human exploration of the Moon since the Apollo programme ended. It costs a huge amount of money to send people there. However, scientists from around the world continue to study the Moon. They use data and samples taken by Apollo spacecraft, rovers and lunar satellites.

NASA's uncrewed Lunar Reconnaissance Orbiter orbits the Moon today. It studies the Moon in great detail. Its findings will help scientists and engineers to plan future lunar landings. Who knows? Maybe you could be part of the next mission to land humans on the Moon!

A future NASA base on the Moon might look like this.

Lunar rovers

Several crewed and robotic vehicles have driven around on the lunar surface to aid scientific studies of the Moon.

Apollo Lunar Roving Vehicle
Astronauts Dave Scott and James Irwin drove the first lunar rover during Apollo 15.

Size:
1.5 m (4.9 ft) long

Weight:
210 kg (465 lb)

Launch date:
26 July, 1971

Lunokhod 2

Part of the Luna 21 mission, this was the Soviet Union's second robotic rover.

Size:
1.35 m (4.5 ft) tall

Weight:
840 kg (1,850 lb)

Launch date:
8 January, 1973

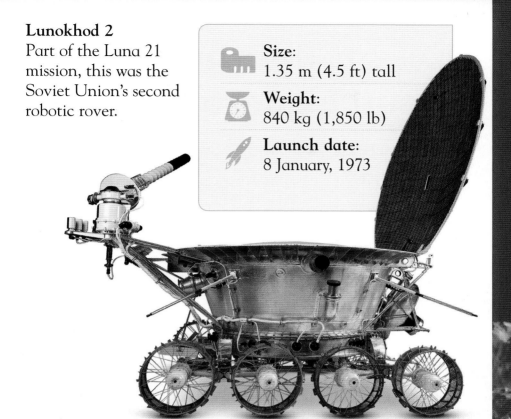

Yutu

This Chinese rover, part of the Chang'e 3 mission, included cameras and technical instruments.

Size:
1.5 m (4.9 ft) tall

Weight:
140 kg (310 lb)

Launch date:
1 December, 2013

Recent international Moon explorations

In recent decades, space agencies from around the world have sent probes to orbit the Moon.

SMART-1 (2003–2006)
The aim of the European Space Agency's SMART-1 satellite was to demonstrate new instrument technologies rather than make scientific discoveries.

Chang'e 1 (2007–2009)
The Chang'e 1 satellite, named after the Chinese lunar goddess, was the first phase of the Chinese Lunar Exploration Programme.

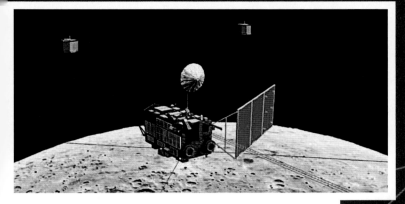

SELENE (2007–2009)
This was the second probe sent to the Moon by Japan. It was nicknamed "Kaguya" and provided detailed maps of the Moon.

Chandrayaan-1 (2008–2009)
Results from the Indian Space Research Organisation's first lunar satellite led to the discovery of water in the Moon's soil.

Quiz

 1   How old is the Moon?

 2   Where is basalt rock found on the Moon?

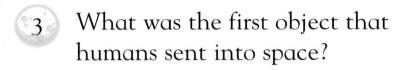 3   What was the first object that humans sent into space?

 4   Which president famously promised to land a man on the Moon?

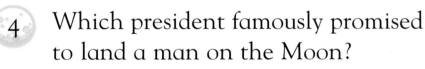 5   On which mission did astronauts first view earthrise?

 6   In which year did Apollo 11 launch?

 7   Who was the first person to set foot on the Moon?

8 Which Apollo mission suffered an explosion on board?

9 Which astronaut played golf on the Moon?

10 Who was the first female engineer at NASA Mission Control?

11 What was the name of the Soviet Union's second robotic lunar rover?

12 What was the name of India's first lunar satellite?

Answers on page 61

Glossary

Apollo
US space agency programme tasked with sending a human to the Moon

astronaut
someone who has trained to fly a spacecraft and work in space

data
information often involving numbers, for example measurements of distance

earthrise
view of the Earth from the Moon

engine
part of a craft that provides power for it to move

lunar
related to the Moon

module
part of a spacecraft

moon
natural satellite orbiting the Earth

NASA
US agency in charge of missions to space – short for National Aeronautics and Space Administration

orbit
move in a circle around something

probe
uncrewed spacecraft that sends information about space back to the Earth

rocket
missile or craft that uses an engine to fly

satellite
object that orbits another

software
programs on a computer that tell it how to perform tasks

spacecraft
vehicle or robotic machine designed to fly through space

Space Race
competition between the US and the Soviet Union to put a human on the Moon

splashdown
when a spacecraft lands in the ocean after returning to the Earth

Index

Aldrin, Edwin "Buzz" 28–29, 34–39

Anders, Bill 18

Apollo 11 26–39

Apollo Lunar Roving Vehicle 48–49, 54

Apollo missions 13, 15–52

Apollo spacecraft 24–25

Armstrong, Neil 28–29, 34–36, 38–39

Bean, Alan 42, 43

Borman, Frank 18

Cernan, Gene 22, 51

Chandrayaan-1 57

Chang'e missions 55, 56

Collins, Michael 28–29, 38–39

Command and Service Module 16–17, 21, 22, 23, 25, 28, 31, 36, 37, 47, 49

Conrad, Pete 42, 43

Cunningham, Walt 16, 17

Duke, Charles 50

Earth 4–5, 51

Earthrise 18, 19

Eisele, Donn 8, 17

engineers 12–13, 41, 44, 53

European Space Agency 56

Gagarin, Yuri 11

Gemini spacecraft 28

Goddard, Robert 13

Haise, Fred 44–45

Hamilton, Margaret 41

Houbolt, John C. 13

Irwin, James 49, 54

Johnson, Katherine 41, 45

Kennedy, John F. 14, 15, 26

Lovell, Jim 18, 44–45

Lunokhod 2 55

Lunar Landing Research Vehicle 30–31

Lunar Module 16, 21, 22, 23, 24, 30, 34, 35, 42, 45

Lunar Reconnaissance Orbiter 53

lunar rovers 48, 52–55

Mitchell, Edgar 47

Moon 4–7

NASA 14–15, 26, 28, 44, 47, 53

Nixon, Richard 38, 39

Northcutt, Poppy 41

O'Hara, Dee 40

Robertson, Billie 40

robotic probes 11, 15, 42, 56–57

rock samples 31, 36, 47, 49, 50

Roosa, Stuart 47

satellites 10–11, 52, 56, 57

Saturn V rockets 13, 18, 22, 24, 25, 27, 32, 33

Schirra, Wally 17

Schmitt, Harrison 51

Schweickart, Rusty 20, 21

scientists 12–13

Scott, David 20, 48, 49, 54

SELENE 57

Shepard, Alan 14, 46–47

SMART-1 56

Soviet Union 10–11, 23, 27, 55

Space Race 10, 23, 27

spacewalks 20, 21

splashdown 25, 31, 37, 45

Sputnik 1 10–11

Stafford, Thomas 22, 23

Swigert, Jack 44–45

Tereshkova, Valentina 12

Tsiolkovsky, Konstantin 12

USA 8–9, 10, 14–52

V-2 rockets 8

von Braun, Wernher 13

Vostok 1 11

women 28, 40–41

Young, John 22, 23, 50

Yutu 55

A LEVEL FOR EVERY READER

This book is a part of an exciting four-level reading series to support children in developing the habit of reading widely for both pleasure and information. Each book is designed to develop a child's reading skills, fluency, grammar awareness and comprehension in order to build confidence and enjoyment when reading.

> **Ready for a Level 3 (Beginning to Read Alone) book**
> A child should:
> * be able to read many words without needing to stop and break them down into sound parts.
> * read smoothly, in phrases and with expression and at a good pace.
> * self-correct when a word or sentence doesn't sound right or doesn't make sense.

A valuable and shared reading experience

For many children, reading requires much effort but adult participation can make reading both fun and easier. Here are a few tips on how to use this book with a young reader:

Check out the contents together:
* read about the book on the back cover and talk about the contents page to help heighten interest and expectation.
* ask the reader to make predictions about what they think will happen next.
* talk about the information he/she might want to find out.

Encourage fluent reading:
* encourage reading aloud in fluent, expressive phrases, making full use of punctuation and thinking about the meaning; if helpful, choose a sentence to read aloud to help demonstrate reading with expression.

Praise, share and talk:
* notice if the reader is responding to the text by self-correcting and varying his/her voice.
* encourage the reader to recall specific details after each chapter.
* let her/him pick out interesting words and discuss what they mean.
* talk about what he/she found most interesting or important and show your own enthusiasm for the book.
* read the quiz at the end of the book and encourage the reader to answer the questions, if necessary, by turning back to the relevant pages to find the answers.

Series consultant, Dr. Linda Gambrell, Emerita Distinguished Professor of Education at Clemson University, has served as President of the National Reading Conference, the College Reading Association and the International Reading Association.